Bayou Stew
An Al-the-Gator Tale

by LaTonya Richardson
Illustrated by Matthew Fields

Bayou Stew
An Al-the-Gator Tale
LaTonya Richardson

FIRST EDITION

ISBN: 978-0-692-15262-1
Library Of Congress Card Number: 2018911093

ALL RIGHTS RESERVED
©2019 LaTonya Richardson

Published in 2019 by LaRich Media Group.
No part of this publication may be translated, reproduced or transmitted in any form or by any means, mechanical, electronic, photocopying, recording, or otherwise, without permission in writing from the author.

For my grandson Jericho whose imagination at three years old, sparked the idea of this book.
- LaTonya

For all the people who support what I do and always push me forward or lift me up. It could not be done without you.
-Matthew

Al-the-Gator woke up from a long, long, ve-e-ery long nap, hungrier than ever before.

Leaving his den in the bayou, Al set out in search of a snack.

Just around the bayou's bend, Al-the-Gator came across Raycoon. "Hey Ray," he said smacking his lips. "My, my, my, how you've grown while I've been asleep. You're looking pretty yummy. Ahem I mean you're looking very healthy these days. Would you like to join me for lunch?"

"Sure, Al," Ray said nervously. "What do you have in mind?"

"I was thinking about a tasty bayou stew my grandma-ma used to make," he said, and then whispered under his breath, "Avec racoon."

"I **love** stew, I'll help you make it."

Al built the fire while Ray collected ingredients.

Soon Al's big pot of boiling water was ready for Ray's mushrooms, slugs, and mudbugs. The two chopped, diced and stirred. Then they stirred some more.

"Have a taste," Ray said, handing Al a spoonful.

Al blew and sipped. "Hmmm, it's missing something," he said, giving Ray a shifty smile.

Ray split, and from a distance yelled: "I'll be right back." Before Al could stir the pot three times, Ray had returned with cypress root and a mess of moss. They chopped, diced and stirred it into the pot.

After a while, Ray suggested that Al "have a taste." And he handed him a ladle full of stew.

Al blew, sipped, and slurped. Smacking his mouth he gave Ray a sly grin.

"Something is missing."

"Stay right there," Ray said, running from Al's den yet again.

Before the bullfrog croaked three times, he was back with arrowhead and algae.

The two chopped, diced, simmered and stirred. Finally, Ray said "Have a taste," and handed Al a cupful of stew.

Al blew, sipped, slurped, and guzzled it all down. Smacking his mouth and almost licking Ray, he announced, "Something is still missing."

Ray ran off one last time.

Before the owl could hoot three times, Ray had returned with an armload of cattails.

"Now this should do the trick," he said.

The two unlikely chums chopped, diced, and stirred the simmering pot of stew.

"Now Al, have a taste." Ray handed him a great big bowlful. Al blew, sipped and slurped, guzzled and gorged till every last drop was gone.

Whatdaya think?"

"I'm so full, and so sleepy I can barely move. But it's still missing a little something." Al burped.

"Missing something you say?" Ray laughed skipping from Al's den.

"Yep, your bayou stew is missing one clever Raycoon."

LaTonya Richardson is an author of picture books for children. Although she loves to cook and eat, she has never eaten raccoon in a stew, or otherwise. LaTonya lives three blocks from Bayou Bartholomew, and has seen her fair share of critters near the bayou, as well as in her yard. She is an instructor at the University of Arkansas at Pine Bluff, and enjoys life with her husband and family.

Matthew Fields is a recent graduate and an experienced professional artist. He is pursuing a Master of Fine Arts in painting and plans to return to his alma mater to work as a professor. He has a passion for art and dream to see creativity be reintergrated into public education.

Bayou Stew, An Al-the-Gator Tale is LaTonya and Matthew's second book together, Going On A Bear Hunt is their previous collaboration.

Visit La'Tonya Richardson's website at
www.larichmedia.com

www.ingramcontent.com/pod-product-compliance
Lightning Source LLC
Chambersburg PA
CBHW061817290426
44110CB00026B/2903